DISCERNING THE DEVIL'S PLAYBOOK

THE FOUR PLAYS FROM NAZI GERMANY CURRENTLY AT PLAY IN AMERICA

MATTHEW MAHER

DISCERNING THE DEVIL'S PLAYBOOK

Published by 55:11 Publishing LLC

1701 Walnut Street 7th Floor | Philadelphia, Pennsylvania 19103 USA

info@5511publishing.com | www.5511publishing.com

55:11 Publishing is committed to Publishing with Purpose. The company reflects the philosophy established by the founders, based on Isaiah 55:11:

"So is My word that goes out from My mouth; it will not return to Me empty, but will accomplish what I desire and achieve the purpose for which I sent it."

Book design copyright © 2024 by 5511 Publishing LLC. All rights reserved.

Interior design & formatting by Landmark Church Creative Department

Cover design by Joanna Sanders LLC, www.colossians46.com

Published in the United States of America

ISBN (Paperback): 978-0-9986306-9-4

DISCERNING THE DEVIL'S PLAYBOOK

THE FOUR PLAYS FROM NAZI GERMANY CURRENTLY AT PLAY IN AMERICA

MATTHEW MAHER

TABLE OF CONTENTS

"INDEED, THE SAFEST

ROAD
TO
HELL

IS THE GRADUAL ONE – THE GENTLE

SLOPE

SOFT UNDERFOOT,

WITHOUT
SUDDEN TURNINGS

WITHOUT
MILESTONES

WITHOUT
SIGNPOSTS... "

C.S. Lewis, Screwtape Letters

Scan to download image
for social media

PREAMBLE

THE ENEMY HAS A LIMITED PLAYBOOK

WITH JUST FOUR PLAYS

HE SUCCESSFULLY RUNS THESE FOUR PLAYS OVER AND OVER AGAIN, AND HAS DONE SO THROUGHOUT THE AGES.

Do you know what they are?

Contradict The Truth

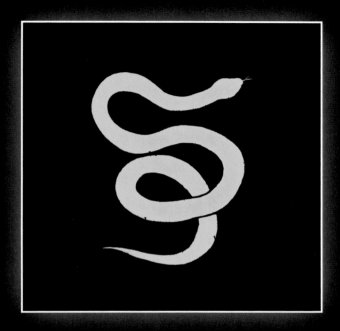

In the Garden of Eden, Satan said to the woman,
"Has God indeed said…" (Genesis 3:1),
which is the timeless question he utilizes
to undermine God and His Word.

Without truth, all hell breaks loose.

Control The News or Narrative

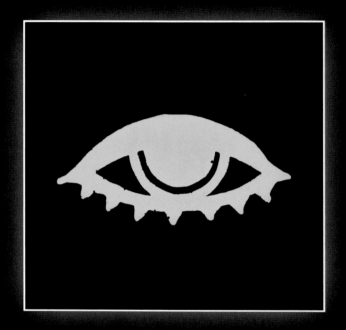

At the Tower of Babel -
"Now the whole earth had one language and
one speech...And they said, 'Come, let us build
ourselves a city, and a tower whose top is in
the heavens; let us make a name for ourselves...'"
(Genesis 11:1,4).

One dictatorial voice of
defiance against the Lord.

Create Conflict To Groups & Nations

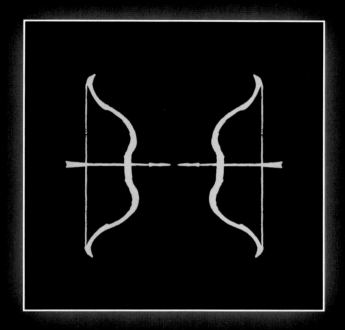

How you are fallen from heaven,
O Lucifer, son of the morning!
How you are cut down to the ground,
you who weakened the nations!
(Isaiah 14:12).

Sow division, reap confusion and destruction.

Convert The Youth

In Babylon, the goal was to teach God's children the language and literature of the Chaldeans, to wipe away any memory of their spiritual legacy (Daniel 1:4). The enemy uses the weapons of mass indoctrination disguised as education.

Immorality packaged as inclusivity.

WE KNOW THAT WE ARE OF GOD AND THE WHOLE WORLD LIES UNDER THE SWAY OF THE WICKED ONE.

1 JOHN 5:19

Scan to download image for social media

In order to not be played by these plays, as believers in the Bible, we must know the truth so well as to readily identify the plays and discern the lies emanating straight from the pit of hell.

Within this short booklet, I want to make seen the unseen by profiling the evil forces that are shaping our land. This booklet seeks to unmask the tactics of the father of lies, which are to distort, deceive, divide, and destroy. But amid "the enemy coming in like a flood, the Spirit of the Lord lifts up a standard against him" (Isaiah 59:19).

And this standard is the weapon of God's Word, the light of His Gospel, and the banner of His truth.

IT MUST BE LIFTED UP!

MIND YOU, THIS

BATTLE

WILL NOT BE WON BY

BALLOTS
OR BULLETS

BUT BY

BIBLICAL
BOLDNESS

Scan to download image for social media

And that is why this booklet serves as a call to arms for believers to not only be aware of the enemy's schemes, but to know that...

"The weapons of our warfare are not carnal but mighty in God for pulling down strongholds, casting down arguments and every high thing that exalts itself against the knowledge of God, bringing every thought into captivity to the obedience of Christ, and being ready to punish all disobedience when your obedience is fulfilled (2 Corinthians 10:4-6)."

"In spiritual war, casual Christians will become casualties"

Scan to download image for social media

Contradict The Truth

PLAY (1)

This is the first step in throwing off God's absolutes. If up is down and down is up, if left is right and right is left, then there are no boundaries and order to be kept. Without divine order determining human order, the result is disorder. Deceivers and liars' traffic in confusion.

Biblical truth matters, for it serves as the divine order that determines human order. Conversely, when the Word of God is not the framework for creative order, the consequential result is disorder. You see, *"where there is no [biblical] revelation, the people cast off restraint"* (Proverbs 29:18). And the enemy knows this, which is why he seeks to counter and contradict the truth of God's absolutes at every turn. From the sacredness of marriage to the standard of morality, and from gender biology to governing authorities, the Adversary's strategy is to contradict or counterfeit what God has established in His Word.

During the rise of Nazi Germany, Adolf Hitler's regime utilized every sector of society as a way to contradict truth and manipulate the masses. His propaganda moved through entertainment and education, media and medicine, politics and pulpits. Joseph Goebbels, Hitler's Minister of Propaganda, famously stated, *"If you tell a lie big enough and keep repeating it, people will eventually come to believe it."* So, with the propaganda machine in full swing, part of their slanderous efforts was to de-Christianize society. In essence, Hitler's "administration" sought to remove God from the conscience of the nation. This he did by neutralizing the church. Hitler said that the churches must be "forbidden from interfering with temporal matters." And God being moved out is the prerequisite for the enemy to move in.

> **"If a ruler pays attention to lies, all his servants become wicked."**
>
> **Proverbs 29:12**

Basically, it was the age-old lie that the sacred and secular must be separate. In the American context, it is the lie of separation of church and state. This concept originates from Thomas Jefferson's letter to the Danbury Baptists, where he spoke of a "wall of separation between church and state," which has since been misapplied to mean a complete exclusion of religious influence from public life. Jefferson's intent was to assure the Danbury Baptists that the government would not be imposing a state religion (i.e., denomination), which was one of the reasons they fled Great Britain. So many in the church are ill-informed or not informed at all about this, and it has led to Christian influence being blocked by a make-believe wall of separation. Ironically, many tout "separation of church and state," but the reality is that there would be no American state without the church.

You see, **the lie of separation of church and state has been weaponized in order to keep the church neutralized**. In addition, the lie of *separation of church and state* always leads to **submission of church to state**, and then eventually **suppression of church by state**. Read that sentence again. It's always in that order.

Likewise in Nazi Germany, churches were suppressed, and religious institutions were co-opted to serve the regime's propaganda machine. Today, we see similar trends with the marginalization and belittling of Christianity in public discourse. **Prayer has been removed from the schoolhouse, the Ten Commandments from the courthouse, and the fear of God from the White House**. Christian values are derided as archaic or intolerant.

Just recently, which serves as a startling marker of where we are as a society, Pastor Jack Hibbs prayed before Congress. Hibbs, who serves as the pastor of Calvary Chapel Chino Hills in California, delivered an opening prayer in the House on January 30th, 2024, which sent a group of "lawmakers" into a rage. The "lawmakers" lamented his comments during the opening prayer as guest chaplain taking issue with the use of the terms "holy fear," "repentance," and

"national sins." Think about that! They were also enraged by Hibbs mentioning God as a Father and Jesus as His Son and our only Savior. As a result, they have labeled Pastor Jack Hibbs as a "radical Christian Nationalist." Couple that with a Politico news pundit who recently said on MSNBC that anyone who believes that God is the giver of our rights, not government, is a Christian Nationalist (more on that term at the end of the booklet).

The words of President Ronald Reagan from a 1984 prayer breakfast are prophetic to this moment: *"Without God, there is no virtue, because there's no prompting of the conscience. Without God, we're mired in the material, that flat world that tells us only what the senses perceive. Without God, there is a coarsening of the society. And without God, democracy will not and cannot long endure. If we ever forget that we're one nation under God, then we will be a nation gone under."*

Again, the large lie of *separation of church and state*, which has been repeated enough for many to falsely come to believe it, has even led the church to stay on the sidelines when we should always be on the frontlines. And without the church on the frontlines, there is no one to defend and define truth. Like history testifies, it was the relentless pressure applied on the church by Hitler and his "lawmakers" that led to the muddying of the waters of truth, which caused the people to drink the poison of lies; willingly and without thinking critically. By suppressing the truth, they paved the way for their nefarious agenda to take hold.

In today's culture, we are witnessing parallel attempts to contradict the truth, often masked under the guise of relativism, progressivism, or even the deceptive allure of socialism. The distortion of fundamental truths about human nature, gender, morality, and sexuality have become prevalent, leading to societal confusion and moral decay. **Think about the fact of how we used to be the land of the free because of the morally brave. Now we are a land in free fall because of the morally broke.**

However, as Christians in these times, it is imperative to stand firm on the truth of God's Word and expose the pervasive lies of the enemy, regardless of the consequences. Like Daniel in Babylon. Like Paul in Rome. Like Dietrich Bonhoeffer in Germany. Like you and I in America. For it is only in the light of truth that we can discern such wickedness and push back the darkness. And if the enemy works through the reprobate minds of evil men to contradict the truth, let us be those who allow the Lord to work through our repentant minds as we constitute the truth.

As the Apostle Paul wrote to Timothy, I likewise exhort you with the same spiritual charge: *"These things I write to you, though I hope to come to you shortly; but if I am delayed, I write so that you may know how you ought to conduct yourself in the house of God, which is the church of the living God, the pillar and ground of the truth"* (1 Timothy 3:14-15).

The influence that can overcome the contradiction of truth is a church that lives by the constitution of truth. Always and in all ways.

> **"The devil abhors light and truth because these remove the ground of his working."**
>
> Watchman Nee

HOW CAN THE ENEMY CONVINCE PEOPLE TO BE COMFORTABLE WITH LIES?

That's the next play.

- - - - - - - - - - - - - - - - - - -

Control The News or Narrative PLAY ②

In a word, propaganda. Hitler once said,
"By means of shrewd lies, unremittingly repeated, it is possible to make people believe that heaven is hell - and hell heaven. The greater the lie, the more readily it will be believed."

Mind you, six corporations control 90% of the media outlets in America. And FYI, none of them espouse a biblical worldview, but even worse, they are hostile to biblical Christianity. Translation, the Marxist mainstream media is lying to you.

The Devil understands the power of information and the influence it holds over the minds of men. He has been at this since the Garden of Eden. Thus, another tactic in his playbook is to seize control of the news, shaping narratives to suit his agenda. Granted, there may not have been "news outlets" before the printing press, but he still worked through *whisper down the lane*, from word of mouth to ear to ear, knowing that lies thrive in the mind when truth is denied. He did the same thing with Nimrod and the Tower of Babel. Man's attempt at controlling the narrative, one voice in opposition to God, led the Lord to confuse their lying efforts.

Again, in Nazi Germany, the Ministry of Public Enlightenment and

Propaganda, led by Joseph Goebbels, exercised total control over the media. Through censorship, propaganda, and manipulation, they monopolized the dissemination of information, ensuring that only their version of reality reached the masses. Sound familiar?

Quotes attributed to Goebbels such as, *"Think of the press as a great keyboard on which the government can play,"* exemplify the extent to which the Nazi regime sought to control the flow of information.

Similarly, in our contemporary landscape, we witness attempts to control the news through censorship, biased reporting, and narrative manipulation. Media conglomerates and tech giants do more than affect public opinion, they are able to alter the consciences and worldviews of entire generations. As already mentioned, six corporations control 90% of the media outlets in America and none of them espouse a biblical worldview.

This is an alarming fact and should serve as a reminder that with the increase of information comes the increase of deception. You can no longer trust many of the "sources" in the media field, the "experts" in the medical field, the "authorities" in the political field, and the "professors" in the academic field. Sadly, even many "pastors" have been nothing but imposters in the spiritual field. I hate to say this, but it is true: **People are sheeple who uncritically accept what's lethal when not shepherded by the Bible.**

Think about how quickly a narrative can sweep a nation and the world. Without having to even bring hard facts to bear, the masses today will accept what they are being told by the Marxist Mainstream Media. The infamous words of Hitler hold true then and now, *"How fortunate for governments that the people they administer don't think."*

For example, within minutes after the death of George Floyd at the end of May of 2020, which went viral through a bystander's recording, the organization of Black Lives Matter had swept the country (and world) like a brush fire being lit by gas. Literally and figuratively. Because that is exactly what it was, a gaslighting of demonic proportions, fueled by the media and followed uncritically by the masses.

In my opinion, and in reference to those specific riots and woke justice outbursts, is that **cities were on fire because pulpits weren't on fire.**

As an aside, isn't it strange that none of us talk about Black Lives Matter anymore? Considering our lives were completely dominated by the subject in 2020. Back then, a headline in The New York Times told us that "Black Lives Matter May Be the Largest Movement in U.S. History." According to Wikipedia, there were upward of 26 million protest participants.

That part may be the only true aspect behind the movement because everything else in the Black Lives Matter narrative begins to fall apart from there. Not only was the organization itself spurred on by Marxist and godless ideologies, but their website originally boasted that it was part of their mission to "disrupt the Western-prescribed nuclear family structure." Translation, destroy the biblical design of the family, built upon two parents, with gender specific roles of a mother and father.

Thus, the BLM organization, aided and abetted by the media, was able to strike a lawless blow to law and order. The "Defund the Police" movement quickly dominated the inner-city streets and the media amplified its impact. It emboldened criminal activity and lawlessness, and oh yeah, all the while the country was supposed to be on lockdown from the imminent threat of the coronavirus. Social distancing and sheltering in place were only for those entities deemed non-essential, like the church. Meanwhile, churches that remained open were smeared by the media as hateful and accused of "not loving one's neighbor." They were prosecuted by their state governments and fined astronomically. Pastors were arrested for simply following the Word of God.

Much more can be said about this entire example, but the point is how controlling the news so easily led to "groupthink," which created a culture where so many weren't thinking. From the Tower of Babel to Nazi Germany's profile, we are living in the days where demonic propaganda is serving the agenda of the Devil.

I know this world is not our home, but the Master I serve told me through His Word to occupy until He returns (Luke 19:13). Thus, as Christians, we must be vigilant consumers of information and data, discerning truth from propaganda. We cannot afford to passively accept the narratives fed to us by the media but must seek out alternative Christian sources whose platforms espouse a biblical worldview, while primarily relying on the discernment granted to us by the Holy Spirit.

Here's a litmus test to see if you should believe the source—if the information you are being told or the position you are taking is also supported by the Marxist Mainstream Media, Big Tech Oligarchy, godless Hollywood, secular Academia, and a political platform that reflects the reprobate minds of Romans 1, I can assure you that you are not on the righteous side of things. Again, one clear indication that your point of view is NOT in alignment with God's Word is when it is supported and affirmed by the non-believing world. And usually, **whatever the world is shouting at the top of their lungs, it is likely that God is whispering the opposite.**

Remember, every field has weeds disguised as seeds and every fold has wolves disguised as sheep. So, I will say it again: **we need to know the truth so well that we can discern the lies of hell.**

And ultimately, if the enemy looks to control people through controlling the news, we as believers ought to be controlled by the Good News which allows the Lord to control our every move. And since God's Word is our authority, we should speak it without apology.

We should speak God's Word with clarity and conviction and leave the consequences to Him. A godless generation cannot tell the Church what we should or shouldn't talk about. In other words, the Church does not need to ask permission to speak righteousness, nor does she need to apologize for exposing darkness. *"And have no fellowship with the unfruitful works of darkness, but rather expose them"* (Ephesians 5:11).

We should be as bold as lions against cowards who propagate lying. We should espouse a biblical worldview in all we do. We should be the salt of the earth and the light of the world as followers of Jesus. We should occupy until He comes. *"Now, Lord, look on their threats, and grant to Your servants that with all boldness they may speak Your word"* (Acts 4:29).

"Silence in the face of evil is itself evil: God will not hold us guiltless. Not to speak is to speak. Not to act is to act."

Widely attributed to Dietrich Bonhoeffer

IF THE "PRINCE OF POWER OF THE AIR" CAN CONTROL THE AIRWAVES,

then he can set the stage which produces the next play...

Create Conflict To Groups & Nations

PLAY ③

> With truth being contradicted and hellish propaganda being propagated, division between people is to be expected. And a people or house divided will inevitably fall, no matter how big or small. If the enemy can get blacks versus whites, rich versus poor, right versus left, then those harnessed by his agenda will likely use such conflict to take more control. Tyrants rise through the vein of lies.

Divide and conquer—a timeless strategy employed by the Devil throughout history. By sowing discord and fostering conflict among groups, he undermines unity and weakens the fabric of society. A house divided against itself cannot stand (Matthew 12:25). This is true for a marriage, a family, a community, a state, a nation, and of course, the church. As the previous chapter alluded to, when lies and deception dominate the news, it is only a matter of time before such chaos brings conflict to groups.

In Nazi Germany, the regime capitalized on existing divisions within society, scapegoating minority groups such as Jews and eventually Christians. Through propaganda that vilified these groups, they stoked fear and resentment among the populace, leading to widespread discrimination and ultimately genocide. This was a slow fade that increased drastically when the people bought in to the lie.

People's false perceptions drove two widely different reactions to their times. In one direction, people turned a blind eye to the atrocities that were happening. On the other hand, many blindly supported wholesale incarceration of Jews because they fell prey to the delusion of a lie—that Jews were somehow a threat to public health and "homeland security." Through deceitful propaganda efforts and controlling the narrative, the government was able to convince the people that Jews were disease carriers. This is what gave rise to

the derogatory slur, a "filthy Jew." Ghettos were designated as quarantine camps, ultimately isolating Jews from society and instilling fear in the population that they could get a disease if they were in contact with a Jew. Sound familiar?

The same ploy was deployed in our land due to the COVID *plandemic*. The government, in tandem with Big Pharma and organizations like the CDC and the WHO, used slogans like "love your neighbor" as propaganda to socially distance or isolate altogether. This led to the push of masks and the vax, and anyone who did not comply was labeled "a threat to society and public safety." As mentioned in the previous chapter, the church was deemed non-essential, meanwhile strip clubs, marijuana dispensaries, bars and nightclubs, big box stores, and many other businesses were allowed to stay open.

Our land has yet to recover from these lies and the conflict that has been leveraged between groups has only widened the division.

Today, we see echoes of this strategy in the societal polarization fueled by identity politics, critical race theory, and intersectionality. *DEI Training*, which has polluted almost every sector of society, uses diversity, equity, and inclusivity as ways to discriminate instead of celebrate. **It's the way of the devil to take something that has a good definition and misappropriate it to bring division**. Evil genius.

In addition to the divisive nature of identity politics and critical race theory, the issue of transgenderism has also become a focal point of contention in society. And not just contention, but it is the manifestation of rebellion against God. So the enemy doubles down and brings further division to that which is already upside down. "*Therefore God also gave them up to uncleanness, in the lusts of their hearts, to dishonor their bodies among themselves, who exchanged the truth of God for the lie, and worshiped and served the creature rather than the Creator, who is blessed forever. Amen*" (Romans 1:24-25).

In present-day America, the case of Jack Phillips, a Colorado baker, provides a vivid example of the divisiveness surrounding LGBTQIA+ rights and pronoun usage. Phillips, a devout Christian, gained national attention when he refused to create a custom cake first for a homosexual couple and then a transgender individual, citing religious objections to supporting their *sexual orientations*. Sadly, the transgender individual only pursued their grievance

to add insult to injury. Phillips was already being upended by the battle he was fighting with the homosexual couple.

These legal battles eventually reached the Supreme Court. While the Court ruled in favor of Phillips based on procedural grounds, the case underscored the deep-seated disagreements over the rights of the LGBTQIA+ community and the limits of religious freedom. This example illustrates how far we have fallen and how Isaiah 5:20 is now the characterization of our culture. *"Woe to those who call evil good, and good evil; Who put darkness for light, and light for darkness; Who put bitter for sweet, and sweet for bitter!"* Woe to those who call a woman a man and a man a woman. Sadly, to even say this publicly is to be labeled a bigot or a hater. And even as of late, the state is willing to bring charges for "hate speech" if you do not bow to the alphabet mafia. **Truthfully, it is not hate speech, it is just speech that they hate.**

All these anti-Christian worldviews are sinister and pit one group against another based on race, gender, or political affiliation, creating fertile ground for animosity and quite frankly, another civil war. In the infamous words of Rahm Emanuel, *"You never let a serious crisis go to waste. And what I mean by that it's an opportunity to do things you think you could not do before."* Sadly, many of these national crises are manufactured by evil leaders to exploit people's fear and uncertainty. This paves the way to advance their agendas, whether it's curtailing civil liberties, silencing dissent, or diverting attention from pressing issues. It's all the same series of plays → contradict the truth, control the news, and thus bring confusion and conflict to groups.

> **"It is an abomination for kings to commit wickedness, for a throne is established by righteousness."**
>
> Proverbs 16:12

As Christians, we are called to be ambassadors of righteousness, not those who bring conflict to groups but those who bring conscience to groups. We are charged by our Lord to be *"the pillar and the ground of the truth"* (1 Timothy 3:15), which makes the Church the conscience of a nation. We do this by not being manipulated by the Devil's playbook, but by operating from God's Book.

> ## "The first step on the way to victory is to recognize the enemy."
>
> ### Corrie Ten Boom

IF ALL THOSE DOMINOES ARE LINED UP,

...he next play that ...

the spoils of war.

- - - - - - - - - - - - - - - - - - -

Convert The Youth

The future of any nation rises or falls on the worldview of the youth. Hitler once said, *"He alone, who owns the youth, gains the future."* Enough said. Now do you see why our children are the target of secular and sexual indoctrination? And if we don't *train* up our children, the world will *tran* up our children; or at the least, if we don't see the importance of biblical truth, the god of this age will put our children in a *trance.*

The future of any nation rises or falls on the worldview of its youth, a reality the Devil understands all too well. Thus, he targets the impressionable minds of young people, seeking to indoctrinate them with his lies and "academic" distortions. He aims his fiery lies at young and impressionable minds, and only the shield of faith can extinguish them.

As Ephesians 6:16 admonishes, *"Above all, taking the shield of faith with which you will be able to quench all the fiery darts of the wicked one."*

Again, consider the quote from Hitler when he said, *"He alone, who owns the youth, gains the future."* This demonic obsession with youth manifested vividly in Nazi Germany. Over the course of the 1930s, the Nazi state abolished all independent youth programs in Germany, paving the way for Hitler to establish a youth organization for the Nazi party known as the Hitler Youth and the League of German Girls. By 1939, more than 82% of eligible youth (ages 10-18) belonged to these organizations, which served as vehicles for the indoctrination of children and adolescents into the ideology of the regime. Through propaganda, militarization, and ideological training, the youth were molded into loyal followers of Hitler's vision.

Today, we witness similar efforts to indoctrinate the youth through education, media, and popular culture. Marxist ideologies disguised as social

justice movements seek to capture the hearts and minds of young people, promoting radical and woke agendas antithetical to biblical truth. **These "brilliant" lies are parroted by political pundits, preached by progressive pastors, and widely presented by "prestigious" professors.**

In addition, the infiltration of Marxist ideologies into educational curricula, particularly in higher education, aims to reshape the worldview of the next generation. Concepts such as critical race theory and gender ideology are increasingly promoted in schools, indoctrinating students with divisive and godless frameworks. This context underscores the alarming escalation of antisemitism on college campuses as of May 2024. To put it bluntly and biblically, in the words of Pastor Gary Hamrick (Cornerstone Chapel in Leesburg, VA), **"Antisemitism is Satanism."** And that is why the emergence of pro-Hamas protests and encampments on university grounds, often likened to *mini*-Gaza's, represents the fruit of this poisonous tree. None of these developments arose overnight; rather, they have simmered within secular academia for decades. The boiling point has been long reached and we are now seeing the disciples of such ignorant worldviews coming to age. **Learned ignorance stands as the most detrimental form of ignorance.**

Sadly, history not heeded is history repeated.

You see, the parallels between the rise of antisemitism in Nazi Germany in 1938 and the current situation on college campuses are eerily similar. In both instances, we witness the propagation of hateful ideologies that demonize and scapegoat Jewish individuals and communities. Much like the systemic discrimination and violence sanctioned by the Nazi regime, the present-day manifestations of antisemitism on campuses have cultivated environments of fear and intimidation that is grossly accepted by the "powers that be" at those universities.

But more than that, to publicly declare a love for "God and country" and a support for the nation of Israel is to be condemned as a racist, a bigot, or a domestic extremist. These dark and demonic ideologies have captured the minds of the next generation in unprecedented numbers.

Furthermore, the present perversion of the LGBTQIA+ agenda plays a significant role in the grooming of children. Under the guise of promoting tolerance and acceptance, children are exposed to explicit sexual content and

encouraged to explore various gender identities at increasingly younger ages. This deliberate desensitization and normalization of deviant behaviors erode traditional values and undermines the moral fabric of society. **A civilization that destroys its youth will eventually destroy itself.**

A war of this magnitude, or as the godless Biden Administration propagated, the battle for the soul of a nation, must be understood by its origins. Throughout history, evidence abounds about the dark forces that have incited civilizations to destroy children. In ancient civilizations, child sacrifice was tragically common, with societies offering their young as appeasement to malevolent deities or to gain favor for their own selfish desires. The Greeks had tales of infanticide and exposure of unwanted children, while the Romans practiced abandonment and even occasional ritualistic killings.

Same demons, different days.

Today, the common assault on children takes subtler forms, from the erosion of traditional family values to the promotion of ideologies that undermine the sanctity of life and the innocence of youth. The normalization of abortion, the push for gender ideology in schools, and the sexualization of children through media and entertainment are all manifestations of this ongoing spiritual battle.

And that is why there is such a relentless effort to label caring parents as "domestic terrorists" for concerning themselves with what their local school boards are allowing into the classrooms or libraries. From pornographic content in literature to encouraging "gender affirming" care without parental consent, we are witnessing the Devil's playbook wreak havoc under the guise of "tolerance."

C.S. Lewis was prophetic when he said, "*Of all tyrannies, a tyranny sincerely exercised for the good of its victims may be the most oppressive.... Those who torment us for our own good will torment us without end for they do so with the approval of their own conscience.... In reality, however, we must face the possibility of bad rulers armed with a Humanitarian theory of punishment....We know that one school of psychology already regards religion as a neurosis. When this particular neurosis becomes inconvenient to government, what is to hinder government from proceeding to "cure" it? Such a "cure" will, of course, be compulsory; but under the Humanitarian theory it will not be called by the shocking name of Persecution.*"

As guardians of the next generation, it is incumbent upon us to recognize these assaults for what they are and to stand firm in protecting the most vulnerable among us from the schemes of the evil one. And that is why the words of Proverbs 22:6 have never been more important and critical: *"Train up a child in the way he should go, and when he is old, he will not depart from it."* As parents, educators, and mentors, it is our solemn responsibility to instill in the youth a foundation grounded in biblical principles, equipping them to discern truth from deception. **It only takes one generation to change the landscape of a nation, for good or for evil.** Thus, we must diligently guard and guide the hearts and minds of our youth, ensuring that they are firmly rooted in the unchanging truth of God's Word.

> **"What one generation tolerates, the next generation will embrace."**
>
> John Wesley

WAKE UP CHURCH!

These plays are currently at play and on the attack. While we have allowed society to remove God, Satan has moved in. And without the Church standing in the way (as the salt of the earth that delays the decay of the day), this antichrist spirit will have its way. The time is now, if we don't return to our biblical foundation, we won't return from this anti-biblical conversion.

Conclusion

As we conclude this examination of the Devil's playbook and its parallels in Nazi Germany, it becomes abundantly clear that the battle for truth and righteousness is as relevant today as it was in ancient times. The schemes of the enemy, though multifaceted and ever-evolving, remain rooted in the same principles of deceit, manipulation, and division. Just as the Apostle Paul exhorted the Ephesian believers to put on the full armor of God to stand against the wiles of the devil, so too are we called to arm ourselves with the truth of God's Word and the discernment of His Spirit (Hebrews 5:12-14).

Throughout history, we have witnessed how the enemy seeks to contradict the truth, control the news, sow conflict among groups, and ultimately convert the youth with antichristian ideologies. From the deception in the Garden of Eden to the propaganda machinery of Nazi Germany, the playbook remains consistent, aimed at undermining God's creative order and leading humanity astray.

Yet, in the face of such darkness, we are not without hope. For as children of light, we are called to shine brightly in the midst of darkness, exposing the deeds of the enemy and proclaiming the liberating truth of the Gospel. May we heed the words of Ephesians 5:8-16:

For you were once darkness, but now you are light in the Lord. Walk as children of light (for the fruit of the Spirit is in all goodness, righteousness, and truth), finding out what is acceptable to the Lord. And have no fellowship with the unfruitful works of darkness, but rather expose them. For it is shameful even to speak of those things which are done by them in secret. But all things that are exposed are made manifest by the light, for whatever makes manifest is light. Therefore He says:

"Awake, you who sleep,
Arise from the dead,
And Christ will give you light."
See then that you walk circumspectly, not as fools but as wise, redeeming the time, because the days are evil.

How does one redeem the time? In the biblical narrative that runs through the Book of Daniel, we find the timeless examples of Daniel, Hananiah, Mishael, and Azariah (famously known as Shadrach, Meshach, and Abednego) that serve as templates of truth regardless of the lies of the times. Remember, the players may be different, but the enemy's plays are always the same.

> ## "Lest Satan should take advantage of us; for we are not ignorant of his devices."
>
> ## 2 Corinthians 2:11

In Daniel chapter 1, we see how the Hebrew boys refused to conform to the Babylonian culture and indoctrination program, even though they were exposed to the "language and literature of the Chaldeans" (Daniel 1:4). That was the primary goal of the Babylonian kingdom, to brainwash the youth so as to make them *clones of culture, parrots of propaganda, puppets of perversion,* and ultimately useful idiots at the disposal of the king's decrees. And yet, Daniel, leading the charge, *"purposed in his heart that he would not defile himself"* (Daniel 1:8).

How were these young boys able to maintain their fidelity of faith even though they were away from home and aliens in a foreign land? The Scriptures don't directly tell us, but **the roots of their courage (over compromise) likely points to their family tree.** Their families must have oriented their consciences around the truth of Scripture, making the enemies attempt to absorb them into the lies of the culture of no effect.

> ## The only way to not be indoctrinated by lies is to be insulated by truth.

Similarly, in Daniel 3, Shadrach, Meshach, and Abednego demonstrated unwavering faith in the face of the *music of the media* (aka the messaging of the day). Despite the decree to bow down to the golden image set up by King Nebuchadnezzar when the music was playing, they refused to compromise their worship of the one true God, even when confronted with the consequence of death. Their refusal to bow serves as a powerful reminder of the importance of standing firm in our convictions, regardless of the consequences.

Additionally, Daniel's steadfastness in Daniel 6 highlights the importance of remaining faithful to the Word of God, regardless of the threat of the jaws of lions or even in the face of jaws that are lying. In Daniel's case, it was both. Despite the decree forbidding prayer to any god or man except King Darius, Daniel continued to pray openly to his God, facing the lion's den as a consequence. Yet, God delivered him, affirming the power of unwavering faith in the face of adversity.

Mind you, when man's law contradicts God's law, civil disobedience is biblical obedience. And we may not get delivered from the *burning fiery furnace* or the *jaws of the lion/lying* like they did, but Jesus is with us in and through the trial.

Incorporating these biblical examples reinforces the timeless principles of the Bible that compel us to resist godless laws, lusts, and leaders. Just as Daniel and his companions remained steadfast in their commitment to God amidst the various ploys deployed from the Devil's playbook, so too are we called to stand firm against the godless pressure by firmly standing on God's power.

> **"You are of God, little children, and have overcome them, because He who is in you is greater than he who is in the world."**
>
> **1 John 4:4**

Therefore, let us not be passive spectators in the face of evil, but active participants in the advancement of God's kingdom on earth. And let us remember that ultimately, the victory has already been won through the death and resurrection of Jesus Christ, who triumphed over sin, death, and the powers of darkness. Thus, let us stand firm as guardians of truth, armed with the knowledge of the enemy's tactics and fortified by the power of God's Word and the examples therein.

To that end, may His truth continue to guard us, His light continue to guide us, and His love continue to grow us as we navigate the texture of our times.

And finally, let us not forget that we were created "for such a time as this." So, what time is this? It's time to stand for timeless truth in the midst of truthless times.

The Spirit of truth forewarns us in order to forearm us.

"However, when He, the Spirit of truth, has come, He will guide you into all truth; for He will not speak on His own authority, but whatever He hears He will speak; and He will tell you things to come" (John 16:13).

As the enemy seeks to **contradict the truth;**

the church must never cease to **constitute the truth.**

As the enemy deceives through **controlling the news;**

the church cannot be deceived when it is **controlled by the Good News.**

As the enemy brings hellish **conflict to groups;**

the church must continue to bring heaven's **conscience to groups.**

As the enemy desires to **convert the youth to be woke;**

the church must remain on fire to **convert the youth to be awake.**

Aftermath

THE SHOT HEARD 'ROUND THE WORLD: A CALL FOR BIBLICAL BOLDNESS IN THE FACE OF NATIONAL CRISIS

The phrase "the shot heard 'round the world" originally described the opening gunfire of the American Revolution, a moment that united a fledgling nation in the pursuit of freedom. Similarly, the bullet that struck President Trump should serve as a catalyst, highlighting the urgent need for Christians to recognize the hour we are in. Just as that historic shot sparked a movement, this event ought to remind believers that this war will not be won by ballots or bullets but by biblical boldness.

The attempted assassination of President Trump on July 13, 2024, is a stark reminder of the present darkness operating in broad daylight and the spiritual battle being waged for the soul of our nation. As outlined in this booklet, the enemy's tactics of contradicting the truth, controlling the news, creating conflict among groups, and converting the youth were on full display in the aftermath of the event. Among the hysteria online were a wide range of responses. From vitriol that went viral about people's disappointment in the shooter missing to those who are convinced the whole thing was just theater, actors playing their patriotic part. These responses and others like them show us the tragic effectiveness of the *Devil's Playbook* and how truth and reality have been hijacked by lies and delusion.

What should have caused everyone to pause and consider the gravity of what occurred seems only to have furthered the divide and fostered even more pride. Pride always goes before destruction; this is true for a person, a church, an organization, and even a nation. The forces at play are beyond human control and require divine intervention. Therefore, we must rise to the occasion, not with fear, but with the confidence that God's providence is at work.

Let the failed assassination attempt on President Trump's life serve as an MRI, helping us honestly assess the ruptured conscience of our nation. There is no way forward without pleading for the Lord's mercy for our national sins and seeking His providential intervention. This is not about making America great, but about making the Lord great in America. Only through faith in the Lord Jesus Christ, heartfelt prayer, and bold proclamation of the gospel can we hope to see true healing and transformation in our nation.

Finally, let us not forget the families whose lives have been forever changed due to the events of July 13, 2024. May our prayers be for those individuals who are grieving the loss of their loved ones, and may the Lord's peace and comfort be upon them. Additionally, may the bullet that grazed the former president's ear be used by God to open his ear. May President Trump humble himself, like Nebuchadnezzar, and see that the Lord's *"dominion is an everlasting dominion, and His kingdom is from generation to generation. All the inhabitants of the earth are reputed as nothing; He does according to His will in the army of heaven and among the inhabitants of the earth. No one can restrain His hand or say to Him, 'What have You done?'"* (Daniel 4:34-35). May this event lead him to repentance, declaring Jesus Christ as Lord and Savior.

This is not about making America great, but about making the Lord great in America.

Addendum A

"Now more than ever the people are responsible for the character of their Congress. If that body be ignorant, reckless, and corrupt, it is because the people tolerate ignorance, recklessness, and corruption. If it be intelligent, brave and pure, it is because the people demand these high qualities to represent them in the national legislature...if the next centennial does not find us a great nation....it will be because those who represent the enterprise, the culture, and the morality of the nation do not aid in controlling the political forces."

James A. Garfield

I find myself wondering how there can be so many conflicting opinions amongst Christians, particularly when it comes to personal views on politics? Politics comes from the Greek word "politikos," meaning, "of, for, or relating to citizens." It originally referred to matters concerning the governance and administration of city-states. Today, it broadly encompasses the activities, processes, and principles associated with governance, power, and decision-making within societies or states.

politikos	meaning: of, for, or relating to citizens

And yet regardless of the diversity of perspectives among Christians on political matters, it's essential at the least to recognize the historical and philosophical underpinnings of Christian influence on governance. And as of late, that is why the rise of the label "Christian Nationalism" is gaining momentum as a pejorative label to disable and undermine the legitimate expression of Christian values in public life. This label seeks to delegitimize Christian influence from government by associating it with extremism or an attempt to impose religious beliefs on others.

Yet, history attests to the foundational role of Christian principles in shaping concepts of liberty, justice, and governance. As Noah Webster, one of America's Founding Fathers, aptly noted, *"The Christian religion... is the basis, or rather the source, of all genuine freedom in government... I am persuaded that no civil government of a republican form can exist and be durable in which the principles of Christianity have not a controlling influence.*" Thus, the labeling of Christian influence in politics as "Christian Nationalism" is a deceptive tactic aimed at eroding the rightful place of Christian values in shaping public policy and discourse. And mark my words, you will begin to see how those who "control the news" will begin to exponentially parrot this term in an effort to disarm Christians from living out their faith in the public space.

There is a dark agenda at work and the contention becomes even more evident as we grapple with the uncertainties and divisions that occur with each upcoming election. Here is a question worth answering: is there a right form of government as God would have it? And before we answer this question specifically and biblically, let's consider the Christian's role in relation to citizenship.

As Christians, we are citizens of heaven (Philippians 3:20), but that doesn't negate our responsibility to participate in our civic responsibility as citizens here on earth (Romans 13:1). A proper exegesis of Romans 13 commands us to engage with our nation's political process (refer back to the quote from James Garfield that served as a superscript to these final thoughts). However, as sojourners, we should operate **solely under a biblical worldview** (not a partisan worldview), which means we affirm that the Bible is the lens through which we view the world and the filter by which every issue of life is run through. And it is in the Word of God where we are commanded to be *salt and light* to the culture around us (Matthew 5: 13-16). Salt engages the decaying culture and preserves it. Light exposes the darkness and overcomes it.

> **"Take away the wicked from before the king, and his throne will be established in righteousness."**
>
> Proverbs 25:5

Now let's consider the question above regarding the Christian's role to government — even in a tyrannical form of it. In the book of Jeremiah, we see a letter written to the Jewish captives to Babylon. It states what the people of God should do while under a godless government: "*And seek the peace of the city where I have caused you to be carried away captive, and pray to the Lord for it; for in its peace, you will have peace"* (Jeremiah 29:7).

Interesting. In the midst of a pagan system, *"Seek the peace of the city where you are placed and pray to the Lord for its peace. Because if the city is at peace, you will have peace."* In other words, if you are the salt of society, then your preserving will lead to humanity flourishing. **Thus, the choice government of God is when God is the choice of government, when His people seek to have Him govern them even in the midst of godless government.** Conversely, to abolish God from government is to allow the government to become god.

Now back to the 21st century.

Isaiah 33:22 states, *"For the Lord is our Judge, The Lord is our Lawgiver, The Lord is our King; He will save us."* Judge. Lawgiver. King.

This verse helps frame the birth of our original governmental structure, where we have a judicial branch (judges), a legislative branch (lawmakers), and an executive branch (president). This separation of powers was intentional to prevent the corruption of power. The founders and framers understood that these 3 branches were offshoots from the trunk of truth (the Bible). You see, from moral law comes the right infrastructure for civil law.

And that is why George Washington stated, *"It is impossible to rightly govern a nation without God and the Bible."* This statement is true even if we were to replace the word nation with "life, or family, or church." It is impossible to rightly govern self without God and the Bible. And if our souls and society are not being governed by the Bible, it is likely because we have been given over to Babel.

You see, when we divorce moral rule from our civil rule, we get arbitrary rule which leads to tyrannical rule. And as Patrick Henry said, *"it is when a people forget God, that tyrants forge their chains."* Tyrants always rise through the vein of lies as 2020 forward has so aptly revealed. **And when the Church and Christian begin to understand their role in our governmental context** (Romans 13:1-7), **we will begin to delay the decay of our day until the Lord pulls us out of the way.** Until then, we are to be the salt and light in our land, which requires us to engage community by praying faithfully, voting biblically, and standing righteously.

The truth of the Gospel saves the soul, and it is Gospel truths that salvage society. As for those who claim to be Christians, we are expected to know **biblical truth and practice what we preach** (2 Timothy 2:15). And without question, it is our responsibility to contribute to the land's Constitutional Republic by voting!

A question I get all the time—*How do I know who to vote for as a Christian? Am I looking for a Christian to lead?* My response is, a Christian should always evaluate the candidate's policies over their personality. And the policy divide and differences have never been more aggressive than they are now. Life versus death. Liberty versus tyranny. Morality versus immorality. Order versus chaos. Truth versus lies. It's the Bible or Babel!

How do I know who to vote for as a Christian?	
Policy Over Personality	
Life vs Death	**Liberty vs Tyranny**
Morality vs Immorality	**Order vs Chaos**
Truth vs Lies	**Bible vs Babel**

Personally, I am not a single-issue voter but a Christian voter. If a party's platform is anti-Christian (pushing out all mention of God), anti-life (they call it pro-choice), anti-Israel (they call it diplomacy), anti-liberty (they call it being progressive), anti-police (they call it reforming society), anti-morality (they call it human rights), and affirms all forms of sexuality, as well as transgenderism, which not only goes against biology, but yes, it goes against biblical theology, then the choice is abundantly and Scripturally clear. There is no nuance to this.

America is at a precipice between freedom and socialism, literally God and godlessness, spiritually and morally. I hope the train of thought in this booklet has opened your eyes to see the war behind the veil. We all must continue to pray for more clarity in these days of depravity. We need *spiritual* eyes to see what is no longer lurking beneath the surface but is blatantly evil and aggressively attacking on all levels — and most specifically aimed at the next generation.

With that being said, my faith compels me to vote biblical because my conscience is held captive to what is Scriptural.

> **"For we must all stand before the judgment seat of Christ, so that each of us may receive what is due us for the things done while in the body, whether good or bad."**
>
> 2 Corinthians 5:10

Addendum B

As I diligently worked on this booklet, several threads jumped off the paper, prompting me to jot them down in a separate document for the possibility of eventually posting as a blog on my website. At that exact time, the term "Christian Nationalism" was being weaponized in the mainstream media (and still is), and that contorted caricature spurred me on to address this issue from a biblical worldview that transcends the political spectrum of right and left. The writing was eventually picked up by *The Washington Times*. Below is that op-ed.

Beyond Left and Right: The Weaponization of Christian Nationalism

As Christians, how we view the world is not confined to the narrow spectrum of right and left but the biblical standards of right and wrong (Hebrews 5:14). Again, our thoughts and actions are not measured on a line of right and left politics but a paradigm of up and down; they are either in alignment with heaven or with hell. The Word or the world (2 Corinthians 2:12-16). And knowing this distinction will keep you from being silenced or intimidated by those who seek to deploy identity politics, using labels or name-games as a weapon of their warfare. **You cannot place a true Christian on a political spectrum because they are partisan to a Person and not to a party**.

For example, in recent years, the term "Christian Nationalism" has been increasingly wielded by "elites" with deceptive motives as a weapon to demonize and marginalize those with traditional Christian values.

The concept of Christian Nationalism is being twisted and distorted to fit a narrative that equates with extremism, bigotry, and authoritarianism. The propaganda machine of the media wants the masses to believe that if you are labeled a Christian Nationalist that it is somehow synonymous with Nazism or fascism. They have deliberately hijacked those words to enjoin them into something sinister.

And here is why this matters! This label seeks to delegitimize Christian influence from government by associating it with extremism or an attempt to impose religious beliefs on others.

Yet, history attests to the foundational role of Christian principles in shaping concepts of liberty, justice, and governance. As Noah Webster, one of America's Founding Fathers, aptly noted, *"The Christian religion... is the basis, or rather the source, of all genuine freedom in government... I am persuaded that no civil government of a republican form can exist and be durable in which the principles of Christianity have not a controlling influence."*

Both the term Christian and Nationalism should not be redefined to paint an evil caricature in our minds. Mind you, they cannot even define "what is a woman," so now we are supposed to accept their definition for "what is a Christian Nationalist?" I will biblically define both, remember, up or down not left or right.

First of all, being a Christian, a follower of Jesus Christ, makes us ambassadors of His Kingdom, sent to represent Him where we are (2 Corinthians 5:20). This does not mean we are trying to make earth heaven, but we are commissioned to bring heaven to earth (Matthew 6:10). We know this world is not our home, but we also know that we are to impact this world until the Lord calls us home (1 Peter 2:11-12).

Thus, a Christian is salt and light (Matthew 5:13-16). Both these agencies bring a heavenward influence to bear. Darkness cannot exist where light chooses to persist. And salt preserves that which would otherwise spoil and pervert. It works as a preservative of righteousness and delays the spreading of unrighteousness. History proves that wherever Christians were active in their faith, it was in that place where society flourished because souls were saved. And a saved soul lives by God's creative order. In other words, they know what is up or down (Romans 12:1-2).

In the Scriptures, we see how God is sovereign over the nations and one day *"every nation, tribe, people, and tongue"* will be represented before the throne (Revelation 5:9-10; 7:9-10). This means God Himself is not for globalism and He clearly has a heart for nationalism. I repeat, *"every nation, tribe, people, and tongues."* Thus, we are called to disciple our nation and its rulers, or we will be discipled by our nation and its rulers. That's a fact.

Ironically (or more like hypocritically), those purveyors of misinformation betray the very values of tolerance, diversity, and inclusivity they tout to their advantage, while actively trying to demonize a large population of our nation. They push tolerance of everything unless you are a Christian that happens to love your nation.

Thus, the labeling of Christian influence in politics as "Christian Nationalism" is a deceptive tactic aimed at eroding the rightful place of Christian values in shaping public policy and discourse. And mark my words, you will begin to see how those who "control the news" will begin to exponentially parrot this term in a deliberate effort to disarm Christians from living out their faith in the public space (John 15:18-19).

Do not let the fear of being called a *Christian Nationalist* silence you— because you unashamedly love your God and have a high esteem for the values that built this country.

The entire Old Testament is God's prerogative and plan for a nation, Israel. His prophetic plan for their redemption is still at work. I guess that makes Him a Nationalist, or dare I say a Zionist. I think you get my point. But to be clear, the New Testament assures us that He wants to make disciples of all nations (Matthew 28:18-20).

Therefore, if the Lord has allowed you to be alive for such a time as this, then live for Christ and impact your nation (Proverbs 25:5). If you don't, then believe me when I say that those who are weaponizing the term Christian Nationalism will continue to remove every trace of what is Christian from this nation. And that is not a right or left thing, that is a heaven versus hell thing.

About the Author

Pictured:

The Maher Family

Matthew, Sarah (wife), Willow (daughter), & Ezekiel (son)

Matthew Maher is a 2007 graduate of Temple University, where he earned his Bachelor of Science degree in Business Administration with a concentration in Legal Studies. He is also a former professional soccer player, playing on teams in North Carolina, New Jersey, and Philadelphia respectively. He is the author of the books: U MAY B THE ONLY BIBLE SOMEBODY READS: R U LEGIBLE?; Imprisoned by Peace: A View Apart; Unchained: A Voice Apart; and Let Us Pray: A Plea Apart (available on Amazon.com).

He is the host of the podcast, Rechurched, aimed at instigating Christians to be Christian, as well as a highly sought-after speaker both on the local and national level. His "Decisions Determine Destiny" program has addressed over 500,000 high school and college students through various events and assemblies.

Matthew is honored to serve as a Pastor at Landmark Church in Ocean City, New Jersey, where his desire is to inspire conscience (so people may know Christ) and instigate conviction (so people may show Christ).

You can learn more at www.TruthOverTrend.com, where his blogs have been read by over 1,000,000 people in every state, 121 countries, and in 67 different languages.

Matthew and his beautiful wife, Sarah, their daughter Willow, and son Ezekiel, reside in Egg Harbor Township, New Jersey.

Social Media | @TruthOverTrend

CONNECT WITH

MATTHEW MAHER

@TruthOverTrend

If you are interested in booking Matthew to speak at your next event or would like to check his availability, visit:

TRUTHOVERTREND.COM

ALSO AVAILABLE FROM
MATTHEW MAHER

U MAY B THE ONLY BIBLE SOMEBODY READS: R U LEGIBLE?
IMPRISONED BY PEACE: A VIEW APART
UNCHAINED: A VOICE APART
LET US PRAY: A PLEA APART

"Thank you for partnering with us in spreading the Gospel."

Matthew Maher

@TruthOverTrend

Spreading the truth in a world of trends.

PUBLISHING

If you enjoyed this book, will you consider sharing the influence with others?

- Share or mention the book on your social media platforms (use images from preamble).

- Encourage your pastor/church to make this resource available to your community.

- Pick up a copy for someone you know who would be spiritually challenged and biblically charged by this message.

- Write a book review on amazon.com.

FOR MORE LITERARY INFLUENCE, PLEASE VISIT:
www.5511publishing.com

Verse-by-verse sermons & studies for you to go deeper in your faith.

thelandmark.church